AF471682

7

Things You Need To Know To Succeed In Life

Terry G. Temple

7 Things You Need to Know to Be a Real Success

ISBN 978-1-300-34836-8

Requests for information, permissions, or orders should be mailed to:

Terry G. Temple
251 Hidden Lake Drive
Powderly, TX 75473-9565

CONTENTS

1—Know That There is a Divine Design 1

2—Know That Everyone is Subject to Authority 9

3—Know What Freedom Really Means and What It Does Not Mean 13

4—Know That You Have Responsibilities 15

5—Know That You Are a Steward, Not an Owner 19

6—Know That You Must Learn to Live With Suffering 23

7—Know The Meaning of Real Success 27

Notes 31

FORWARD

There is a culture war raging in this nation. This war is for the kind of society in which we live, but also for the souls of our children.

Although it has always been important to teach our children the foundational values of Christianity and of our country, it is even more crucial that parents do so today.

I urge parents to teach these things to their children beginning at an early age, and to reinforce them as they grow to maturity.

Parenting in today's world presents the greatest challenge in the lives of adults. There are many influences attempting to draw our children away from the ultimate truths found in the Christian foundations upon which our nation was founded, and which governed the culture of this nation for the first 200 years of its existence.

I pray that this brief book will be of assistance in focusing on some essential truths each child should know and believe. Of course, if a person does not know Jesus Christ as Lord and Savior of his life, anything else known, experienced, or accomplished on this earth is of no value.

1

Know That There is A Divine Design

God, the Creator of all things, has a design for everything—for the Universe, for mankind, and for each of us individually.

God's Design for the Universe

"In the beginning God created the heavens and the earth."—Genesis 1:1

There can be no more straightforward statement about the creation than this verse, and there can be no more important statement for any person who claims to be a disciple of Jesus Christ. This statement from the Word of God is accepted as fact by those of us who believe in the true and living God. We believe this by faith; **it cannot be proven by science.** Oh, and by the way, **it cannot be disproven by science.**

Our Creator God established a system of laws by which His creation would function. Since the creation, these laws have controlled and sustained His creation.

Those of another worldview choose to believe that the Creation occurred without any intelligent Designer. In this view, the Cosmos either has always existed, or that there was a "Big Bang" resulting in the Cosmos coming into being.

Along with this theory of cosmic existence, there is the theory of Darwinian evolution having to do with life on Earth. This "theory" (it does not meet the scientific definition of a theory), taught primarily through public education systems and college science departments, is an attempt to explain the origin of life without the existence of a divine being. Believers in this hypothesis contend that humans are the product of random mutations of properties already existing in matter, and that man evolved through a series of these mutations over a period of millions or billions of years. **This is a theory based on faith.** It **cannot be proven by science**. Ironically, it **can be disproven by science.**

The laws of science that govern the Universe should be enough to disprove the error of the Darwinian Theory. For example:

- This "theory" is in direct opposition to the Second Law of Thermodynamics, which says in effect that all systems, left to themselves, move from a state of order to disorder (entropy). The Darwinian Theory teaches that man evolved from a state going from disorder to order.
- Mutations are actually an enemy of the Darwin's theory. Mutations result in an inferior creature, rather than an improved one. Mutations are usually sterile—unable to reproduce themselves (example: the mule). Instead of an explanation of the origin of life, mutations are actually examples of the origin of death and disease.

- Nothing in the earth's fossil record has yielded transitional life forms (missing links) to support Darwin's theory. All such "finds" by so-called scientists have later been proven to be either a man or an ape or a hoax—not a transitional life form.
- The discovery of DNA, and subsequent research, has discredited Darwin's theory, and has given credibility to the biblical account of the creation of mankind. The animal kingdom continues to follow God's command in Genesis 1:24: *"Let the earth bring forth the living creature according to its kind: cattle and creeping thing and beast of the earth, each according to its kind"; and it was so.*

God established a grand design for the Universe. He established the laws by which it operates. Such laws make up **true science.** No scientific laws contradict the *Bible.* In fact, where the *Bible* speaks of scientific matters, it is scientifically correct.

Today many scientists believe in the creation, or in what they like to call Intelligent Design. Many others recognize that the Darwinian Theory is totally false, but hold onto it as the only alternative to recognizing the existence of the Creator.

God's Design for Mankind

God also has a plan for humankind. He created us for fellowship with Him. This is the reason that mankind innately desires to worship God. If a person refuses to worship God, he substitutes something else as the object of his worship.

God wants us, as His ultimate creation, to desire an intimate relationship with Him. He could have created us to function as robots, only able to do what is programmed into us, but in His sovereignty He chose to give us the will to decide to accept or reject such a relationship. We each choose whether we will worship and fellowship with Him. He longs for us to choose fellowship with Him.

In His eternal knowledge, our Creator knew even before the creation that the very first man, Adam, would choose to disobey His commandments, and by doing so, bring sin into the world. As his descendants, we inherited Adam's sinful nature.

God also knew before the creation which of us would choose to accept the plan by which He wants to bring redemption to humanity. His plan was and is to accomplish our redemption through the work of God the Son (Jesus) on the cross of Calvary.

God's redemption of mankind is the theme of the entire *Bible.*

God's Design for Individuals

In addition to God's plan for all mankind, He has an individual plan for each unique human being. We are created in His likeness, and are treasured by Him.

His will for our individual lives is communicated to us by the Holy Spirit as we communicate with Him in prayer and in the study of His written Word—the *Bible*. God's plan for our lives is revealed to us day by day. We do not wake up one day and suddenly know every detail of God's plan for us. We may know the overall work to which He has called us, but the plan for each of our days is revealed as we walk with Him each day. God reveals these details to us through:

- Principles we learn from the *Bible;*
- Advice from godly counselors (pastors, parents, teachers, etc.);
- Common sense; and,
- Our own desire to do His will.

There may be times when none of these seem to make things clear to us; but, in most cases, a disciple who thoroughly searches God's Word will find the basis for an intelligent decision.

God's design for our lives began before we were born (see Psalms 139:13-16). These verses tell us that God formed our inward parts (soul and spirit), and that we are "fearfully and wonderfully made (physically). It further tells us that God "saw my substance, being yet unformed," and that in His book were written all the days He fashioned for us.

There is one thing God included in His plan for every human being—that we choose to have the relationship of a child to Him through faith in Jesus Christ. 2 Peter

3:9 tells us that God does not want "any to perish, but that all should come to repentance."

Once we have become a disciple, God plans for us to become more and more like Jesus as we go through the lifelong process of sanctification. God wills for us to be "conformed to the image of His Son."[i]

God has also designed a system of standards for what is right and wrong—**His moral law**. We find the basic framework for these standards in what is commonly called "The Ten Commandments," or "The Decalogue."[ii] These are eternal—they will never change. Sinful men who want to justify living outside the law of God are always trying to do away with them, but God's standards do not change.

The laws of Western Civilization are based on the Decalogue. The United States of America was founded as a Christian country, and the laws of our country have historically been consistent with God's laws.

However, beginning with Franklin D. Roosevelt, liberal anti-Christian Presidents, congressmen, and judges began a concerted effort to undermine the very laws that have made this the greatest and most blessed country in the world.

Jesus gave us the guidelines for Christian living in His "Sermon on the Mount."[iii] He tells us we are to even love those who are ungodly. Some people today use His words as the basis for calling Christians intolerant when we do not accept sinful behaviors. It is important to know that Jesus set the example for us by loving sinners, but hating their sinful lifestyles.[iv] We can love a sinful person, but that does not make it necessary to accept their sinful lifestyles. When Jesus forgave the woman caught in the act of adultery, He told her to "Go, and sin no more." Jesus does not teach us either by word or deed that we must accept lifestyles that violate God's moral laws.

2

Know That Everyone is Subject to Authority

As a part of His creation, God established a system of authority for the effective functioning of individuals, families, and communities (from local to global).

Each of us is accountable to higher authorities, and this accountability remains in place for the entirety of our lives. Nobody is exempt from such accountability.

If a person does not come to understand this, his or her life will always be filled with trouble. Our prisons are full, and will likely remain so, because many individuals refuse to accept this fact of life.

God is the ultimate authority to which each of us is accountable. As Creator, He has the right to make the rules by which we are to live our lives. The fact that we may not like some of His standards does not change the fact that we are accountable to Him for the way we live the lives He has given us.

Authority Within the Family

The family is the first institution God established. The family consists of a man, his wife, and any children with which God has blessed them.

Within the family, God placed a system of authority. God ordained that **the husband** be head of the household, and He laid on him some very awesome responsibilities. He is to:

- Love his wife "as Christ loved the church, and gave Himself for it";
- Be the spiritual leader of the family;
- Train the children to reverence God by teaching them His Word; helping them come to know Him as Lord and Savior as they reach the age of accountability; and, by teaching them to keep His commandments.

The husband/father will give an account to God for how he fulfills these responsibilities.

God made **the wife** to be the 'helpmeet' for her husband—helping him to accomplish the things for which he is responsible. Together, they are to provide a loving, nurturing home for the family.

Together as **parents**, God delegated the husband and wife authority over their children. **Children** are to be obedient to their parents in all things, with only two exceptions:

1. Children are not required to obey instructions that violate the moral laws of God; and,
2. Children are not required to obey instructions of any law of government that is contrary to God's law.

The Authority of Government

God established **governments** as His instruments to execute justice. He delegated to them the authority to enforce civil and criminal law, and to punish offenders.[v] This includes the right to carry out capital punishment, when necessary.

As Christians, we only have the right to disobey a law if it is in conflict with God's moral laws (see endnote ii).

Authority in the Workplace

Bosses have authority in the workplace. As employees, we should give our employers an honest day's work for a day's pay. We should respect our employers, carry out their instructions, and try to help them make their organization a success. If we find we cannot do this, we should find another employment situation.

Authority in Schools

Teachers have authority at school. Parents are ultimately responsible for teaching their children, but if children are enrolled in either a private or public school, teachers have the delegated authority from the parents while the child is at school. Parents must work cooperatively with teachers to ensure the academic success of their children.

Parents should **never totally delegate spiritual and moral instruction** to the schools! Parents are ultimately responsible for these areas of instruction.

Individual Authority

As **individuals**, we make choices every day that chart the course of our lives. These life-changing decisions are made early in life. Children and young people today make decisions that affect them for the rest of their lives. They have to make many more such choices than I did as a youth. I tremble when I look back on some of the decisions I made, and the alternatives I could have chosen. In His grace, God protected me from myself in many cases.

We must realize early in life that we should not make some choices hastily or impulsively. Unhealthy choices made at an early age can diminish or destroy our lives.

In our day-to-day lives, we may often find ourselves in a position of authority. It may be as a parent, a teacher, a coach, a supervisor, etc. Regardless of the role, we need to know how to appropriately use the authority that comes with the position.

Lifetime Subjection to Authority

To reiterate, we will **always** be subject to authority! Regardless of our role—whether we are a child, student, parent, boss, teacher, or President of the United States—we will be accountable to a higher authority.

We will never reach a point in life when we are not accountable to someone, or some entity. As a teacher, I have heard students express their desire to be out of school so they would nor longer have to answer to anybody for anything. That attitude will result in a life of failure

Even if it were possible to not be accountable to anybody, we are all ultimately accountable to God.

3

Know What Freedom Really Means, And What It Does Not Mean

The concept of freedom is seriously misunderstood in this country. As an example, when I was a young man there was a hit song by the Mamas and Papas, the lyrics being:

> "You've got to go where you want to go,
> "Do what you want to do,
> "With whomever you want to do it."

This clearly expresses most people's concept of freedom. Wrong!

Freedom is not doing whatever we like whenever we like! That is anarchy and lawlessness, not freedom.

God has established boundaries of acceptable behavior for us in His Word—the *Holy Bible*. Many people view His boundaries as being restrictive—and they are. God has placed restrictions upon us just as any loving parent places restrictions on the behaviors and activities of their children.

Why do loving parents say "No" to a child? It is for one of two reasons (or possibly both). These are:

1. To protect the child from danger and probable harm, or
2. Because they are aware of better choices or alternatives.

When God says “No” to us, it is for the very same reasons.

As a well-known writer has said, “Behind every negative commandment in the *Bible* are two positive principles: One is to *protect* us; the other is to *provide for* us.[vi]

Freedom has another essential ingredient, and that is **self-discipline**. A free country can remain free only if its citizens are willing to submit to the boundaries of acceptable behavior established by God and by their government. We must recognize that there are things we must not do because of its negative affect on others.

Our freedom as Christians comes from the submission of our wills to the will of Christ. When we do that, we find that we have the liberty to do things that bring joy and happiness to ourselves and those around us.

Within a family, freedom includes submitting to each other in love. There are times when we may want to do one thing, but others in the family have other ideas. We need to consider others as we exercise our freedom.

4

Know That You Have Responsibilities

RESPONSIBILITY—this is a dirty word in our current day and age; however, we should realize that freedom and responsibility go hand in hand.

Parents should begin to teach children responsibility at a very early age. Children should be given greater responsibilities as they grow up. They should be taught that as they show they can handle responsibilities, they are given more freedom; that increased freedom brings with it more responsibilities.

We have responsibilities in all aspects of our life.

Responsibilities to God, Our Creator

As members of the "family of God," we have the responsibility of knowing Him intimately. We get to know Him in this way by reading His Word, by communicating with Him in prayer, and by allowing the Holy Spirit to guide us in our thoughts and actions (the Holy Spirit will never lead us to any action that is contrary to the *Bible*).

The *Bible* is God's **complete revelation** of Himself to mankind. We can know God through His Word, and may approach Him directly without any other person interceding for us. The *Bible* tells us that Jesus is our high priest, and that we can come boldly before God's throne of grace where Christ is interceding for us (Hebrews, chapter 7).

As we nurture our relationship with Him, God enables us to fulfill our other responsibilities as His disciples. These include, but are not limited to:

- Allowing the Holy Spirit to transform us into the image of Christ, as He leads us through the life-long process of sanctification.
- Presenting our bodies to Him as a living sacrifice. This means that we reflect His love to a world filled with hate; reflect His light (truth) to a world filled with spiritual darkness (lies and deception; and, reflect His life to a world filled with death.
- Loving our fellow Christian disciples. We do this because Christ commands it.
- Reaching out to unbelievers. Jesus goal was to "seek and to save" the lost. We do this by sharing our testimony with our unsaved friends and by sharing the Gospel with them. We have the responsibility of actively carrying out the Commission He gave us to spread the Good News to the entire world.
- Worshipping the Lord individually, and with other believers as members of a local assembly of disciples.

We have the responsibility to live our lives in a way that brings honor to the family of God.

Responsibilities to Our Family

As children, family responsibilities include such things as loving our parents and siblings; obeying our parents; learning the things they try to teach us; doing our share of household chores, etc.

As adults, our family responsibilities include such things as establishing a loving and nurturing home for our spouse and our children; providing food clothing and shelter for our family; and teaching our children the way of God by our example.

Each family member should conduct themselves in such a way that we do not bring dishonor or disgrace on our family.

We should practice unconditional love for members of our family, just as God has such love for us. This love is defined for us in 1 Corinthians 13:4-8:

"Love is patient and kind. Love is not jealous, it does not brag, and it is not proud. Love is not rude, is not selfish, and does not get upset with others. Love does not count up the wrongs that have been done. Love is not happy with evil, but is happy with the truth. Love patiently accepts all things. It always trusts, always hopes, and always remains strong. Love never ends."

There will be times when we **will not like the behavior** of another member of our family, but we must always love that person.

Responsibilities to Society

We have responsibilities as members of society. We have the responsibility to be good citizens, actively participating in our government. This involves:

- Knowing the issues that are being addressed, or need to be addressed, by our government;
- Informing our elected representatives of our opinion regarding these issues;
- Being informed about those seeking public office, and knowing their position on the issues;
- Voting whenever we have the opportunity;
- Seeking public office, if we are qualified and think we are able to perform the duties of that office;
- Abiding by the laws of our country, state, county, city, etc., as long as they do not require us to violate the laws of God; and,
- Working to overturn laws at any level of our government that are contrary to the laws of God.

5

Know That You Are a Steward, Not an Owner

God created all things. He owns everything—we own nothing.

You and I came into this world with nothing, and we will leave this world with nothing. God blesses us with material goods during our lifetime, and allows us to manage them.

God gave mankind stewardship of our world, our lives, our families, and our material possessions. The way we conduct our lives should reflect the fact that we are only managers, not owners.

We are responsible for managing the world God created for us. In Genesis 1:26, God said, "Let Us make man in Our image, according to our likeness. They will rule over the fish of the sea, the birds of the sky, the livestock, **all the earth**, and the creatures that crawl on the earth." I fear that we have failed to do a proper job of managing the earth because of our selfish and destructive tendencies.

We are responsible for managing our time. God gives it to us, and we should manage it wisely. We can best do this by investing our time in things that have eternal value.

We are responsible for managing our families. The family is the first institution God established. Within this institution, God allows us the privilege of parenthood, and gives us the responsibility of rearing our children to know Him, and to have the proper awe and respect for Him because of who He is.

We are responsible for management of our material possessions—food, clothing, homes, cars, and all the other 'stuff' with which we are blessed. God has blessed us far beyond the level of our basic needs. We are to use these resources to further God's eternal purposes, and to bless others who are in need.

Because we have become a selfish, greedy, ravenous nation of consumers, we are in danger of becoming the economic slaves of godless countries. We have become dependent upon China for manufactured goods; upon the Islamic countries of the Middle East for our petroleum needs; upon countries of South America and Asia for our shoes and clothing;, and the list goes on.

This is important because it affects our ability to wisely use our resources as God intended.

God holds us accountable for our management of all this and we will answer to Him for the way we used the resources with which He blessed us. We will receive, or fail to receive, eternal rewards for our management of the things He owns.

When we die, we will leave behind all the 'things' we have accumulated in this brief life, and it will pass on to someone else for them to manage.

What is our real legacy? It is not how much money or property we leave to our descendants. **Our real legacy is the influence we have on the lives of those who survive us. That is our only real legacy.**

6

Know That You Must Learn to Live With Suffering

Adam and Eve brought sin into this world by their disobedience. Along with sin, they also brought the penalties of suffering and death to all mankind.

Suffering is a part of the life experience for everyone. Job 14:1-2 state this clearly. *"All of us born to women live only a few days and have lots of trouble. We grow up like flowers, then dry up, and die. We are like a passing shadow that does not last."*

People often ask questions like these:

- "Why does God allow all this evil?"
- "Why does He allow bad things to happen to good people?"
- "If there is a God, why does He not do away with evil?"

The answer is that humankind, with the sinful nature we inherited from Adam, has brought about the evil in the world.

God has provided a remedy for this. If **all of mankind** would accept the redemption offered through Christ's death for our sins, and if we would then live according to His standards, then we would live in a completely different world.

There would be no tyrants such as Adolph Hitler, Joseph Stalin, Saddam Hussein, etc.: however, we would still have suffering as individuals as the result of the Adamic curse on mankind. As a result of "The Fall," suffering is a part of the human experience.

Christians have always suffered persecution, and that is the case in today's world. In many other countries, our Christian brothers and sisters have historically endured torture and martyrdom for their faith, and that is true today more than at any time in the history of the world.

In the past, Christians in the United States have not been persecuted for our Christian faith. Since this country was founded by people who were strong Christians, or who had a firm foundation in biblical values, Christianity was the norm. Sadly, this is no longer the case in this country.

The founders of this country were, for the most part, Christians; and, those who did not consider themselves Christian lived by and strongly encouraged biblical values as the underpinning of the country they were creating. The historical document of this country, along with the writings of the founders, proves this to be correct.

However, during the 1930s, socialist and communist thought was introduced into our government through the programs of Franklin D. Roosevelt's "New Deal."

This trend was furthered by the Roosevelt-appointed Supreme Court's "loose interpretation" of our nation's basic document, the Constitution. Now, the Christian values and ethics that have made this country great are being eroded by court rulings. The Supreme Court has stepped outside the judicial sphere, has made law through its rulings, and by doing so has invaded the sphere of the legislative branch of government.

What has been the legacy of F.D.R.'s socialist activism? Hostility has increased in the United States toward Christ, and toward those who consider themselves true followers of Christ.

Persecution of Christians has always existed in most of the world, but it is a recent phenomenon in the U. S. In the past, persecution has been subtle and more social in nature; but one only has to watch the daily news on television to see that persecution is beginning to be more overt.

As an example, historically-held Christian values and ethics are at the point of being "criminalized." For example, preaching that homosexuality is sin (which is evident to anyone studying the Bible) is moving toward becoming defined as a hate crime. God plainly gives His thoughts on this subject (see Leviticus 18:22; Leviticus 20:13; and Romans 1:24-32).

It may be that soon true practicing Christians can expect to suffer in the same way our brothers and sisters in other lands have suffered for their faith. If so, we should count it a privilege. Jesus warned us that "People will insult you and hurt you. They will lie and say all kinds of evil things about you because you follow Me. But when they do, rejoice and be glad, because you have a great reward waiting for you in Heaven."[vii]

We should have the attitude of the early disciples when persecuted for the cause of Christ. "The apostles left the meeting full of joy because they were given the honor of suffering disgrace for Jesus."[viii]

7

Know the Real Meaning of Success

The humanistic value system under the control of Satan would have us believe that success is measured by three things:

- **Self-indulgence** (pleasing our fleshly senses);
- **Materialism** (amassing money and possessions);
- **Status** (social standing and perceived 'power').

The wide acceptance of these world values are expressed in these bumper stickers that are, or have been, popular:

"If it feels good, do it"
"The person who dies with the most toys wins"
"My child is an honor student at ______"
"My kid can beat up your honor student"

The Bible instructs us to reject these values in defining success in this life. 1 John 2:15-17 is specific in giving us this warning.

There is nothing wrong with enjoying the blessing God has given us—food, clothing, shelter, physical pleasures in their proper context, money, material blessings or prominent roles in society. However, they become sin when we make them the primary focus of our life.

God's Word says, "The love of money is the root of all evil."[ix] The warning is not to **love** (or **live for**) the accumulation of money. Money is necessary for doing business, paying our debts, and buying the things we need to live. It is when we cease to see it as a tool for our use and we begin to live for the purpose of making more that it becomes sin. At that point, it has ceased working for us, and we have become its slave.

When we become enslaved by self-indulgence, money and possessions, or status, it has become our god, and that is the sin of idolatry.

Real success is measured by whether we are living in a proper relationship with God.

1. Are we committed to being His disciple?
2. Are we communing with Him daily through prayer and the study of His Word?
3. Are we applying what we learn as we conduct our daily activities?
4. Are we allowing Him to transform us into the image of Jesus Christ (sanctification)?

These are the things that define whether we are truly successful in this life.

If we have the proper relationship with Christ, then it follows that we will have the proper relationship with others—our spouse, our children, our relatives, our boss, our friends, etc.

Most people never find true success because they lack the essential relationship with their Creator. They live their entire life pursuing happiness, and never finding it because they build their lives on the central belief that happiness is the primary reason for our existence.

Remember this—**Happiness is the by-product of living in the will of God.** If one lives in this way, one will suddenly discover that happiness is theirs.

Notes

---

[i] Romans 8:29
[ii] Exodus 20:1-17 and Deuteronomy 5:6-21
[iii] Matthew, chapters 5-7
[iv] John 8:2-11
[v] Romans 13:1-7
[vi] Josh McDowell and Dick Day, *Why Wait? What You Need to Know About the Teen Sexuality Crisis* (San Bernadino, CA: Here's Life Publishers, Inc., 1987), page 190.
[vii] Matthew 5:11-12
[viii] Acts 5:41
[ix] 1 Timothy 6:10

www.ingramcontent.com/pod-product-compliance
Ingram Content Group UK Ltd.
Pitfield, Milton Keynes, MK11 3LW, UK
UKHW041902190726
13854UKWH00003B/1049